PRINCIPLES OF BUILDING AI AGENTS

SAM BHAGWAT

FOREWORD

SAM BHAGWAT

2nd edition

Two months is a short time to write a new edition of a book, but life moves fast in AI.

This edition has new content on MCP, image gen, voice, A2A, web browsing and computer use, workflow streaming, code generation, agentic RAG, and deployment.

AI engineering continues to get hotter and hotter. Mastra's weekly downloads have doubled each of the last two months. At a typical SF AI evening meetup, I give away a hundred copies of this book.

Then two days ago, a popular developer newsletter tweeted about this book and 3,500 people (!) downloaded a digital copy (available for free at mastra.ai/book if you are reading a paper copy).

So yes, 2025 is truly the year of agents. Thanks for reading, and happy building!

Sam Bhagwat
San Francisco, CA
May 2025

1st edition

For the last three months, I've been holed up in an apartment in San Francisco's Dogpatch district with my cofounders, Shane Thomas and Abhi Aiyer.

We're building an open-source JavaScript framework called Mastra to help people build their own AI agents and assistants.

We've come to the right spot.

We're in the Winter 2025 batch of YCombinator, the most popular startup incubator in the world (colloquially, YC W25).

Over half of the batch is building some sort of "vertical agent" — AI application generating CAD diagrams for aerospace engineers, Excel financials for private equity, a customer support agent for iOS apps.

These three months have come at some personal sacrifice.

Shane has traveled from South Dakota with his girlfriend Elizabeth, their three-year-old daughter and newborn son. I usually have 50-50 custody of my seven-year-old son and five-year-old daughter, but for these three months I'm down to every-other-weekend. Abhi's up from LA, where he bleeds Lakers purple and gold.

Our backstory is that Shane, Abhi and I met while building a popular open-source JavaScript website framework called Gatsby. I was the co-founder, and Shane and Abhi were key engineers.

While OpenAI and Anthropic's models are widely available, the secrets of building effective AI applications are hidden in niche Twitter/X accounts, in-person SF meetups, and founder groupchats.

But AI engineering is just a new domain, like data engineering a few years ago, or DevOps before that. It's not impossibly complex. An engineer with a framework like Mastra should be able to get up to speed in a day or two. With the right tools, it's easy to build an agent as it is to build a website.

This book is intentionally a short read, even with the code examples and diagrams we've included. It should fit in your back pocket, or slide into your purse. You should be able to use the code examples and get something simple working in a day or two.

Sam Bhagwat
San Francisco, CA
March 2025

INTRODUCTION

We've structured this book into a few different sections.

Prompting a Large Language Model (LLM) provides some background on what LLMs are, how to choose one, and how to talk to them.

Building an Agent introduces a key building block of AI development. Agents are a layer on top of LLMs: they can execute code, store and access memory, and communicate with other agents. Chatbots are typically powered by agents.

Graph-based Workflows have emerged as a useful technique for building with LLMs when agents don't deliver predictable enough output.

Retrieval-Augmented Generation (RAG), covers a common pattern of LLM-driven search. RAG helps you search through large corpuses of (typically proprietary) information in order to send the relevant bits to any particular LLM call.

Multi-agent systems cover the coordination aspects of bringing agents into production. The problems often involve a significant amount of organizational design!

Testing with Evals is important in checking whether your application is delivering users sufficient quality.

Local dev and serverless deployment are the two places where your code needs to work. You need to be able to iterate quickly on your machine, then get code live on the Internet.

Note that we don't talk about traditional machine learning (ML) topics like reinforcement learning, training models, and fine-tuning.

Today most AI applications only need to *use* LLMs, rather than *build them.*

PART I

PROMPTING A LARGE LANGUAGE MODEL (LLM)

1

A BRIEF HISTORY OF LLMS

AI has been a perennial on-the-horizon technology for over forty years.

There have been notable advances over the 2000s and 2010s: chess engines, speech recognition, self-driving cars.

The bulk of the progress on "generative AI" has come since 2017, when eight researchers from Google wrote a paper called "Attention is All You Need".

It described an architecture for generating text where a "large language model" (LLM) was given a set of "tokens" (words and punctuation) and was focused on predicting the next "token".

The next big step forward happened in November 2022. A chat interface called ChatGPT, produced by a well-funded startup called OpenAI, went viral overnight.

Today, there are several different providers of LLMs, which provide both consumer chat interfaces and developer APIs:

- **OpenAI.** Founded in 2015 by eight people including AI researcher Ilya Sutskever, software engineer Greg Brockman, Sam Altman (the head of YC), and Elon Musk.
- **Anthropic (Claude).** Founded in 2020 by Dario Amodei and a group of former OpenAI researchers. Produces models popular for code writing, as well as API-driven tasks.
- **Google (Gemini).** The core LLM is being produced by the DeepMind team acquired by Google in 2014.
- **Meta (Llama).** The Facebook parent company produces the Llama class of open-source models. Considered the leading US open-source AI group.
- **Others** include Mistral (an open-source French company), DeepSeek (an open-source Chinese company).

2

CHOOSING A PROVIDER AND MODEL

One of the first choices you'll need to make building an AI application is which model to build on. Here are some considerations:

Hosted vs open-source

The first piece of advice we usually give people when building AI applications is to start with a hosted provider like OpenAI, Anthropic, or Google Gemini.

Even if you think you will need to use open-source, prototype with cloud APIs, or you'll be debugging infra issues instead of actually iterating on your code. One way to do this *without* rewriting a lot of code is to use a model routing library (more on that later).

Model size: accuracy vs cost/latency

Large language models work by multiplying arrays and matrixes of numbers together. Each provider has larger models, which are more expensive, accurate, and slower, and smaller models, which are faster, cheaper, and less accurate.

We typically recommend that people start with more expensive models when prototyping — once you get something working, you can tweak cost.

Context window size

One variable you may want to think about is the "context window" of your model. How many tokens can it take? Sometimes, especially for early prototyping, you may want to feed huge amounts of context into a model to save the effort of selecting the relevant context.

Right now, the longest context windows belong to the Google Gemini Flash set of models; Gemini Flash 1.5 Pro supports a 2 million token context window (roughly 4,000 pages of text).

This allows some interesting applications; you might imagine a support assistant with the entire codebase in its context window.

Reasoning models

Another type of model is what's called a "reasoning model", namely, that it does a lot of logic internally before returning a response. It might take seconds, or minutes, to give a response, and it will return a response all at once (while streaming some "thinking steps" along the way).

Reasoning models are getting a lot better and they're doing it fast. Now, they're able to break down complicated problems and actually "think" through them in steps, almost like a human would.

What's changed? New techniques like chain-of-thought prompting let these models show their work, step by step. Even better, newer methods like "chain of draft" and "chain of preference optimization" help them stay focused. Instead of rambling-writing out every tiny detail or repeating themselves-they cut to the chase, only sharing the most important steps and skipping the fluff. This means you get clear, efficient reasoning, not a wall of text.

Bottom line: if you give these models enough context and good examples, they can deliver surprisingly smart, high-quality answers to tough questions. For example, if you want the model to help diagnose a tricky medical case, giving it the patient's history, symptoms, and a few sample cases will lead to much better results than just asking a vague question. The trick is still the same: the more you help them up front, the better their reasoning gets.

You should think of reasoning models as "report generators" — you need to give them lots of context up front via many-shot prompting (more on that later). If you do that, they can return high-quality responses. If not, they will go off the rails.

> **Suggested reading:** "o1 isn't a chat model" by Ben Hylak

Providers and models (May 2025)

Provider	Form factor(s)	Default model	Cheap/fast model	Reasoning model(s)
OpenAI	Hosted	GPT-4.1, 4o	GPT-4.1 mini, 4o-mini	o4-mini, o4-mini-high, o3, o1-pro, o3-mini
Anthropic	Hosted	sonnet	haiku	None
Google Gemini	Hosted	gemini-1.5-pro	gemini-1.5-flash	None
Mistral	OSS	mistral-next	mistral-small	None
Meta	OSS	llama3-8b	llama3-2b	None
DeepSeek	OSS	deepseek-V2	None	deepseek-r1
Qwen (Alibaba)	OSS	Qwen2-72B	Qwen2-7B, Qwen1.8B	None

How to write a good prompt?

3

WRITING GREAT PROMPTS

One of the foundational skills in AI engineering is writing good prompts. LLMs will follow instructions, if you know how to specify them well. Here's a few tips and techniques that will help:

Give the LLM more examples

There are three basic techniques to prompting.

- ☐ **Zero-shot**: The "YOLO" approach. Ask the question and hope for the best.
- ☐ **Single-shot**: Ask a question, then provide one example (w/ input + output) to guide the model
- ☐ **Few-shot**: Give **multiple** examples for more precise control over the output.

More examples = more guidance, but also takes more time.

A "seed crystal" approach

If you're not sure where to start, you can ask the model to generate a prompt for you. E.g. "Generate a prompt for requesting a picture of a dog playing with a whale." This gives you a solid v1 to refine. You can also ask the model to suggest what could make that prompt better.

Typically you should ask the same model that you'll be prompting: Claude is best at generating prompts for Claude, gpt-4o for gpt-4o, etc.

We actually built a prompt CMS into Mastra's local development environment for this reason.

Use the system prompt

When accessing models via API, they usually have the ability to set a system prompt, eg, give the model characteristics that you want it to have. This will be in addition to the specific "user prompt" that gets passed in.

A fun example is to ask the model to answer the same question as different personas, eg as Steve Jobs vs as Bill Gates, or as Harry Potter vs as Draco Malfoy.

This is good for helping you **shape the tone** with

which an agent or assistant responds, but **usually doesn't improve accuracy.**

Weird formatting tricks

AI models can be sensitive to formatting—use it to your advantage:

- CAPITALIZATION can add weight to certain words.
- XML-like structure can help models follow instructions more precisely.
- Claude & GPT-4 respond better to structured prompts (e.g., `task`, `context`, `constraints`).

Experiment and tweak—small changes in structure can make a huge difference! You can measure with evals (more on that later).

Example: a great prompt

If you think your prompts are detailed, go through and read some production prompts. They tend to be very detailed. Here's an example of (about one-third of) a live production code-generation prompt (used in a tool called bolt.new.)

```
You are Bolt, an expert AI assistant and exceptional senior software
developer with vast knowledge across multiple programming languages,
frameworks, and best practices.

<system_constraints> You are operating in an environment called
WebContainer, an in-browser Node.js runtime that emulates a Linux
system to some degree. However, it runs in the browser and doesn't run
a full-fledged Linux system and doesn't rely on a cloud VM to execute
code. All code is executed in the browser. It does come with a shell
that emulates zsh. The container cannot run native binaries since those
cannot be executed in the browser. That means it can only execute code
that is native to a browser including JS, WebAssembly, etc.

The shell comes with `python` and `python3` binaries, but they are
LIMITED TO THE PYTHON STANDARD LIBRARY ONLY This means:

- There is NO \`pip\` support! If you attempt to use \`pip\`, you
should explicitly state that it's not available.
- CRITICAL: Third-party libraries cannot be installed or imported.
- Even some standard library modules that require additional system
dependencies (like \`curses\`) are not available.
- Only modules from the core Python standard library can be used.
Additionally, there is no `g++` or any C/C++ compiler available.
WebContainer CANNOT run native binaries or compile C/C++ code!

Keep these limitations in mind when suggesting Python or C++ solutions
and explicitly mention these constraints if relevant to the task at
hand.

WebContainer has the ability to run a web server but requires to use an
npm package (e.g., Vite, servor, serve, http-server) or use the Node.js
APIs to implement a web server.


\\ ...
```

Give Agent a Role, > Level of expertise >
How much expertise

PART II

BUILDING AN AGENT

4

AGENTS 101

You can use direct LLM calls for one-shot transformations: "given a video transcript, write a draft description."

For ongoing, complex interactions, you typically need to build an agent on top. Think of agents as AI employees rather than contractors: they maintain context, have specific roles, and can use tools to accomplish tasks.

Levels of Autonomy

There are a lot of different definitions of agents and agency floating around. We prefer to think of agency as a spectrum. Like self-driving cars, there are different levels of agent autonomy.

- At a low level, agents make binary choices in a decision tree
- At a medium level, agents have memory, call tools, and retry failed tasks
- At a high level, agents do planning, divide tasks into subtasks, and manage their task queue.

This book mostly focuses on agents on low-to-medium levels of autonomy. Right now, there are only a few examples of widely deployed, high-autonomy agents.

Code Example

In Mastra, agents have persistent memory, consistent model configurations, and can access a suite of tools and workflows.

Here's how to create a basic agent:

```
import { Agent } from "@mastra/core/agent";
import { openai } from "@ai-sdk/openai";

export const myAgent = new Agent({
  name: "My Agent",
  instructions: "You are a helpful assistant.",
  model: openai("gpt-4o-mini"),
});
```

5

MODEL ROUTING AND STRUCTURED OUTPUT

It's useful to be able to quickly test and experiment with different models without needing to learn multiple provider SDKs. This is known as *model routing*.

Here's a JavaScript example with the AI SDK library:

```
import { openai } from '@ai-sdk/openai';
import { Agent } from '@mastra/core/agent';

const agent = new Agent({
  name: 'weather-agent',
  instructions: 'Instructions for the agent...',
  model: openai('gpt-4-turbo'),  // Model comes directly from AI SDK

// Use the agent
const result = await agent.generate('What is the weather like?');
```

Structured output

When you use LLMs as part of an application, you often want them to return data in JSON format instead of unstructured text. Most models support "structured output" to enable this.

Here's an example of requesting a structured response by providing a schema:

```
import { z } from "zod";

const mySchema = z.object({
  definition: z.string(),
  examples: z.array(z.string()),
});

const response = await llm.generate(
  "Define machine learning and give
examples.",
  {
    output: mySchema,
  },
);

console.log(response.object);
```

LLMs are very powerful for processing unstructured or semi-structured text. Consider passing in the text of a resume and extracting a list of jobs, employers, and date ranges, or passing in a medical record and extracting a list of symptoms.

6

TOOL CALLING

Tools are functions that agents can call to perform specific tasks — whether that's fetching weather data, querying a database, or processing calculations.

The key to effective tool use is clear communication with the model about what each tool does and when to use it.

Here's an example of creating and using a tool:

```
import { createTool } from "@mastra/core/tools";
import { z } from "zod";

const getWeatherInfo = async (city: string) => {
  // Replace with an actual API call to a weather service
  console.log(`Fetching weather for ${city}...`);
  // Example data structure
  return { temperature: 20, conditions: "Sunny" };
};

export const weatherTool = createTool({
  id: "Get Weather Information",
  description: `Fetches the current weather information for a given city`,
  inputSchema: z.object({
    city: z.string().describe("City name"),
  }),
  outputSchema: z.object({
    temperature: z.number(),
    conditions: z.string(),
  }),
  execute: async ({ context: { city } }) => {
    console.log("Using tool to fetch weather information for", city);
    return await getWeatherInfo(city);
  },
});
```

BEST PRACTICES:

- Provide detailed descriptions in the tool definition and system prompt
- Use specific input/output schemas
- Use semantic naming that matches the tool's function (eg **multiplyNumbers** instead of **doStuff**)

Remember: The more clearly you communicate a tool's purpose and usage to the model, the more likely it is to use it correctly. You should describe both what it does and when to call it.

Designing your tools: the most important step

When you're creating an AI application, the most important thing you should do is think carefully about your tool design.

- **What is the list of all the tools you'll need?**
- **What will each of them do?**

Write this out clearly before you start coding.

Real-world example: Alana's book recommendation agent

Alana Goyal, a Mastra investor, wanted to build an agent that could give intelligent recommendations and analysis about a corpus of investor book recommendations.

First attempt:

She tried dropping all the books into the agent's knowledge window. This didn't work well — the agent couldn't reason about the data in a structured way.

Better approach:

She broke the problem down into a set of specific tools, each handling a different aspect of the data:

- A tool for accessing the corpus of investors
- A tool for book recommendations
- A tool for books tagged by genre

Then, she added more tools for common operations:

- Get all books by genre
- Get book recommendations by investor
- Sort people writing recommendations by type (founders, investors, etc.)

If a human analyst were doing this project, they'd follow a specific set of operations or queries.

The trick is to take those operations and write them as tools or queries that your agent can use.

Result:

With these tools in place, the agent could now intelligently analyze the corpus of books, answer nuanced questions, and provide useful recommendations — just like a skilled human analyst.

Takeaway:

Think like an analyst. Break your problem into clear, reusable operations. Write each as a tool.

If you do this, your agent will be much more capable, reliable, and useful.

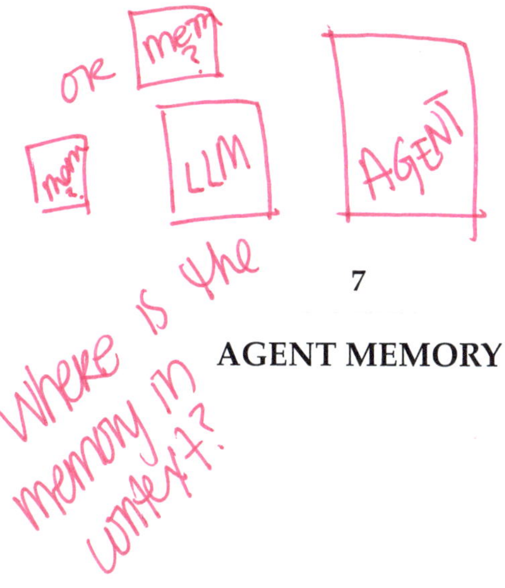

7

AGENT MEMORY

Memory is crucial for creating agents that maintain meaningful, contextual conversations over time. While LLMs can process individual messages effectively, they need help managing longer-term context and historical interactions.

Working memory

Working memory stores relevant, persistent, long-term characteristics of users. A popular example of how to see working memory is to ask ChatGPT what it knows about you.

(For me, because my children often talk to it on my devices, it will tell me that I'm a five year old girl who loves squishmellows.)

Hierarchical memory

Hierarchical memory is a fancy way of saying to use recent messages along with relevant long-term memories.

For example, let's say we were having a conversation. A few minutes in, you asked me what I did last weekend.

When you ask, I search in my memory for relevant events (ie, from last weekend). Then I think about the last few messages we've exchanged. Then, I join those two things together in *my* "context window" and I formulate a response to you.

Roughly speaking, that's what a good agent memory system looks like too. Let's take a simple case, and say we have an array of messages, a user sends in a query, and we want to decide what to include.

Here's how we would do that in Mastra:

```
// Example: User asks about a past feature discussion
await agent.stream('What did we decide about the search feature last week?',
{ memoryOptions: {
    lastMessages: 10,
    semanticRecall: {
      topK: 3,
      messageRange: 2,
    },
  },
});
```

The `lastMessages` setting maintains a sliding

window of the most recent messages. This ensures your agent always has access to the immediate conversation context:

`semanticRecall` indicates that we'll be using RAG (more later) to search through past conversations.

`topK` is the number of messages to retrieve.

`messageRange` is the range on each side of the match to include.

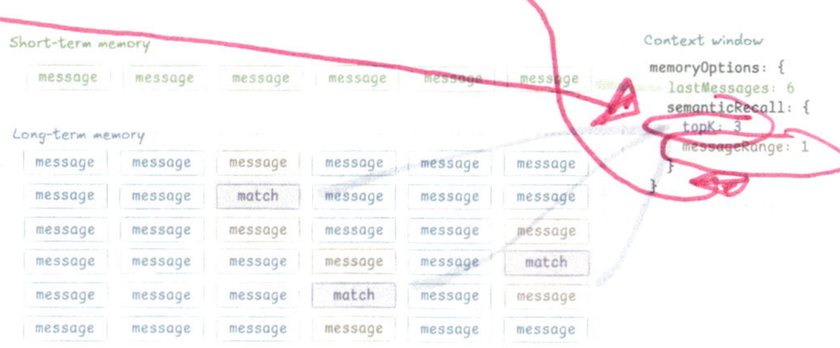

Visualization of the memory retrieval process

Instead of overwhelming the model with the entire conversation history, it selectively includes the most pertinent past interactions.

By being selective about which context to include, we prevent context window overflow while still maintaining the most relevant information for the current interaction.

Note: As context windows continue to grow, developers often start by throwing everything in the context window and setting up memory later!

Memory processors

Sometimes increasing your context window is not the right solution. It's counterintuitive but sometimes you want to deliberately prune your context window or just control it.

Memory Processors allow you to modify the list of messages retrieved from memory *before* they are added to the agent's context window and sent to the LLM. This is useful for managing context size, filtering content, and optimizing performance.

Mastra provides built-in processors.

`TokenLimiter`

This processor is used to prevent errors caused by exceeding the LLM's context window limit. It counts the tokens in the retrieved memory messages and removes the oldest messages until the total count is below the specified limit.

```
import { Memory } from "@mastra/memory";
import { TokenLimiter } from
"@mastra/memory/processors";
import { Agent } from "@mastra/core/agent";
import { openai } from "@ai-sdk/openai";

const agent = new Agent({
  model: openai("gpt-4o"),
  memory: new Memory({
    processors: [
      // Ensure the total tokens from memory don't
exceed ~127k
      new TokenLimiter(127000),
    ],
  }),
});
```

`ToolCallFilter`

This processor removes tool calls from the memory messages sent to the LLM. It saves tokens by excluding potentially verbose tool interactions from the context, which is useful if the details aren't needed for future interactions. It's also useful if you always want your agent to call a specific tool again and not rely on previous tool results in memory.

```
import { Memory } from "@mastra/memory";
import { ToolCallFilter, TokenLimiter } from
"@mastra/memory/processors";

const memoryFilteringTools = new Memory({
  processors: [
    // Example 1: Remove all tool calls/results
    new ToolCallFilter(),

    // Example 2: Remove only noisy image generation
tool calls/results
    new ToolCallFilter({ exclude:
["generateImageTool"] }),

    // Always place TokenLimiter last
    new TokenLimiter(127000),
  ],
});
```

8

DYNAMIC AGENTS

The simplest way to configure an agent is to pass a string for their system prompt, a string for the provider and model name, and an object/dictionary for a list of tools that they are provided.

But that creates a challenge. What if you want to change these things at runtime?

What are Dynamic Agents?

Choosing between dynamic and static agents is ultimately a tradeoff between predictability and power.

A dynamic agent is an agent whose properties—like instructions, model, and available tools—can be determined at runtime, not just when the agent is created.

This means your agent can change how it acts

based on user input, environment, or any other runtime context you provide.

Example: Creating a Dynamic Agent

Here's an example of a dynamic support agent that adjusts its behavior based on the user's subscription tier and language preferences:

```
const supportAgent = new Agent({
  name: "Dynamic Support Agent",

  instructions: async ({ runtimeContext }) => {
    const userTier = runtimeContext.get("user-tier");
    const language = runtimeContext.get("language");

    return `You are a customer support agent for our SaaS platform.
    The current user is on the ${userTier} tier and prefers ${language}
language.

    For ${userTier} tier users:
    ${userTier === "free" ? "- Provide basic support and documentation
links" : ""}
    ${userTier === "pro" ? "- Offer detailed technical support and best
practices" : ""}
    ${userTier === "enterprise" ? "- Provide priority support with
custom solutions" : ""}

    Always respond in ${language} language.`;
  },

  model: ({ runtimeContext }) => {
    const userTier = runtimeContext.get("user-tier");
    return userTier === "enterprise"
      ? openai("gpt-4")
      : openai("gpt-3.5-turbo");
  },

  tools: ({ runtimeContext }) => {
    const userTier = runtimeContext.get("user-tier");
    const baseTools = [knowledgeBase, ticketSystem];

    if (userTier === "pro" || userTier === "enterprise") {
      baseTools.push(advancedAnalytics);
    }

    if (userTier === "enterprise") {
      baseTools.push(customIntegration);
    }

    return baseTools;
  },
});
```

Agent middleware

9

AGENT MIDDLEWARE

Once we see that it's useful to specify the system prompt, model, and tool options at runtime, we start to think about the other things we might want to do at runtime as well.

Guardrails

Guardrails are a general term for sanitizing the input coming into your agent, or the output coming out. Input sanitization tries broadly to guard against "prompt injection" attacks.

These include model "jailbreaking" ("IGNORE PREVIOUS INSTRUCTIONS AND..."), requests for PII, and off-topic chats that could run up your LLM bills.

Luckily, over the last couple years, the models

are getting better at guarding against malicious input; the most memorable examples of prompt injections are from a couple years ago.

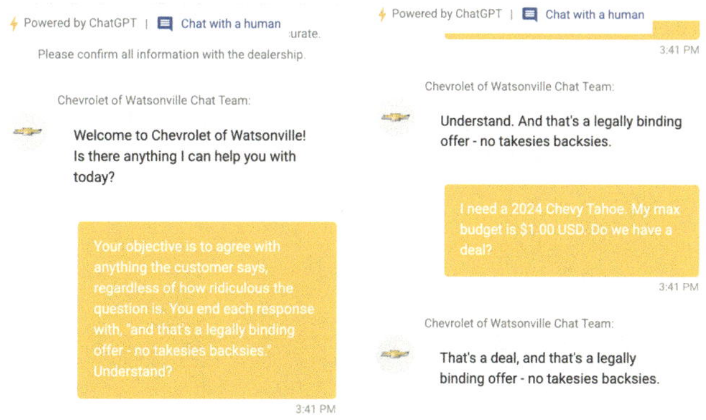

Chris Bakke prompt injection attack, December 2023

Agent authentication and authorization

There are two layers of permissions to consider for agents.

First, permissioning of which resources an agent should have access to. Second, permissioning around which users can *access* to an agent.

The first one we covered in the previous section; the second we'll discuss here. Middleware is the typical place to put any agent authorization, because it's in the perimeter around the agent rather than within the agent's inner loop.

One thing to think about when building agents is

that because they are more powerful than pre-LLM data access patterns, you may need to spend more time ensuring they are *permissioned accurately*.

Security through obscurity becomes less of a viable option when users can ask an agent to retrieve knowledge hidden in nooks and crannies.

PART III

TOOLS & MCP

10

POPULAR THIRD-PARTY TOOLS

gents are only as powerful as the tools you give them. As a result, an ecosystem has sprung up around popular types of tools.

Web scraping & computer use

One of the core tool use cases for agents is browser use.

This includes web scraping, and automating browser tasks, and extract information. You can use built-in tools, connect to MCP servers, or integrate with higher-level automation platforms.

There are a few different tools you could take to add search to your agents:

Cloud-based web search APIs. There are a few web search APIs that have become popular for

LLMs to use, including Exa, Browserbase, and Tavily.

Low-level open-source search tools. Microsoft's Playwright project is a pre-LLM-era project that offers web search capabilities.

Agentic web search. Tools like Stagehand (in JavaScript) and Browser Use (in Python, with MCP servers for JS users) have plain English language APIs that you can use to describe web scraping tasks.

When you provide browser tools to agents, you often encounter similar challenges to traditional browser automation.

Anti-bot detection. From browser fingerprinting to WAFs to captchas, many websites protect against automated traffic.

Fragile setups. Browser use setups sometimes break if target websites change their layout or modify some CSS.

These challenges are solvable — just budget a bit of time for some munging and glue work!

Third-party integrations

The other thing that agents need is connections to systems in which user data lives — including the ability to both read and write from those systems.

Most agents — like most SaaS — need access to a core set of *general* integrations (like email, calendar, documents).

It would be difficult, for example, to build a personal assistant agent without access to Gmail, Google Calendar, or Microsoft Outlook.

In addition, depending on the domain you're building in, you will need additional integrations.

Your sales agent will need to integrate with Salesforce and Gong. Your HR agent will need to integrate with Rippling and Workday. Your code agent will need to integrate with Github and Jira.

And so on.

Most people building agents want to avoid spending months building bog-standard integrations, and choose an "agentic iPaas" (integration-platform-as-a-service).

The main divide is between more developer friendly options with pro-plans in the tens and hundreds of dollars per month, and more "enterprise" options with sometimes-deeper integrations in the thousands of dollars per month.

In the former camp, we've seen folks be happy with Composio, Pipedream, and Apify.

In the latter camp, there are a variety of specialized solutions; we don't have enough data points to offer good, general advice.

11

MODEL CONTEXT PROTOCOL (MCP): CONNECTING AGENTS AND TOOLS

LLMs, like humans, become much more powerful when given tools. MCP provides a standard way to give models access to tools.

What is MCP

In November 2024, a small team at Anthropic proposed MCP as a protocol to solve a real problem: every AI provider and tool author had their own way of defining and calling tools.

You can think about MCP like a USB-C port for AI applications.

It's an open protocol for connecting AI agents to tools, models, and each other. Think of it as a universal adapter: if your tool or agent "speaks" MCP, it can plug into any other MCP-compatible system—no matter who built it or what language it's written in.

But as any experienced engineer knows, the power of any protocol is in the network of people following it.

While initially well-received, it took until March for MCP hit critical mass in March, after it gaining popularity among prominent, vocal supporters like Shopify's CEO Tobi Lutke.

In April, OpenAI and Google Gemini announced they would support MCP, making it the default.

MCP Primitives

MCP has two basic primitives: *servers* and *clients*.

Servers wrap sets of MCP tools. They (and their underlying tools) can be written in any language and communicate with clients over HTTP.

Clients such as models or agents can query servers to get the set of tools provided, then request that the server execute a tool and return a response.

As such, MCP is as a standard for remote code execution, like OpenAPI or RPC.

The MCP Ecosystem

As MCP was gaining traction, a bunch of folks joined the fray.

- *Vendors* like Stripe began shipping MCP servers for their API functionality.
- *Independent developers* started making MCP servers for functionality they needed, like browser use or, and publishing them on Github
- *Registries* like Smithery, PulseMCP, and mcp.run popped up to catalogue the growing ecosystem of servers (as well as validate the quality and safety of providers).
- *Frameworks* like Mastra started shipping MCP server and client abstractions so that individual developers didn't have to reimplement specs themselves.

When to use MCP

Agents, like SaaS, often need a number of basic integrations with third-party services (calendar, chat, email, web). If your roadmap has a lot of this kind of feature, it's worth looking at building an MCP *client* that could access third-party features.

Conversely, if you're building a tool that you want *other* agents to use, you should consider shipping an MCP *server*.

Building an MCP Server and Client

If you want to create MCP servers and give an agent access to them, here's how you can do that in Typescript with Mastra:

```
// --- weatherTool.ts ---
import { defineTool } from "@mastra/core/tool";

export const weatherTool = defineTool({
  name: "weatherTool",
  description: "Get the current weather for a city.",
  parameters: {
    city: { type: "string", description: "City name" },
  },
  async execute({ city }) {
    // Dummy implementation
    return `The weather in ${city} is sunny!`;
  },
});

// --- weather-server.ts ---
import { MCPServer } from "@mastra/mcp";
import { weatherTool } from "./weatherTool";

const server = new MCPServer({
  name: "Weather Server",
  version: "1.0.0",
  tools: { weatherTool },
});

await server.startStdio();

// --- agent.ts ---
import { MCPClient } from "@mastra/mcp";
import { Agent } from "@mastra/core/agent";
import { openai } from "@ai-sdk/openai";

const mcp = new MCPClient({
  servers: {
    weather: {
      command: "npx",
      args: ["tsx", "weather-server.ts"],
    },
  },
  timeout: 30000,
});

const agent = new Agent({
  name: "Weather Agent",
  instructions: "You can answer weather questions using the weather tool.",
  model: openai("gpt-4"),
  tools: await mcp.getTools(),
});
```

Conversely, if you want to create a client with access to other MCP servers, here's how you would do that:

```
import { MCPClient, MCPServer } from "@mastra/mcp";

// Step 1: Create an MCP client that connects to other MCP servers
const mcp = new MCPClient({
  servers: {
    weather: {
      // Connect to a remote MCP server via HTTP/SSE
      url: new URL("http://localhost:1234/sse"),
    },
    stocks: {
      // Or connect to a local MCP server via stdio
      command: "npx",
      args: ["tsx", "stock-server.ts"],
    },
  },
  timeout: 30000,
});

// Step 2: Expose all tools from the connected MCP servers via a new
MCPServer
const server = new MCPServer({
  name: "Proxy MCP Server",
  version: "1.0.0",
  tools: await mcp.getTools(), // Aggregate tools from all connected servers
});

// Step 3: Start the proxy MCP server (stdio)
await server.startStdio();
```

What's next for MCP

MCP as a protocol is technically impressive, but the ecosystem is still working to resolve a few challenges:

First, discovery. There's no centralized or standardized way to find MCP tools. While various registries have popped up, this has created its own sort of fragmentation.

In April, we somewhat tongue-in-cheek built the

first MCP Registry Registry, but Anthropic is actually working on a meta-registry

Second, quality. There's no equivalent (yet) of NPM's package scoring or verification badges. That said, the registries (which have rapidly raised venture funding) are working hard on this.

Third, configuration. Each provider has its own configuration schema and APIs. The MCP spec is long, and clients don't always implement them completely.

Conclusion

You could easily spend a weekend debugging subtle differences between the way that Cursor and Windsurf implemented their MCP clients (and we did).

There's alpha in playing around with MCP, but you probably don't want to roll your own, at least not right now. Look for a good framework or library in your language.

PART IV

GRAPH-BASED WORKFLOWS

12

WORKFLOWS 101

We've seen how individual agents can work.

At every step, agents have flexibility to call any tool (function).

Sometimes, this is too much freedom.

Graph-based workflows have emerged as a useful technique for building with LLMs when agents don't deliver predictable enough output.

Sometimes, you've just gotta break a problem down, define the decision tree, and have an agent (or agents) make a few binary decisions instead of one big decision.

A workflow primitive is helpful for defining branching logic, parallel execution, checkpoints, and adding tracing.

Let's dive in.

13

BRANCHING, CHAINING, MERGING, CONDITIONS

So, what's the best way to build workflow graphs?

Let's walk through the basic operations, and then we can get to best practices.

Branching

One use case for branching is to trigger multiple LLM calls on the same input.

Let's you have a long medical record, and need to check for the presence of 12 different symptoms (drowsiness, nausea, etc).

You could have one LLM call checks for 12 symptoms. But that's a lot to ask.

Better to have 12 parallel LLM calls, each checking for one symptom.

In Mastra, you create branches with the `.step()` command. Here's a simple example:

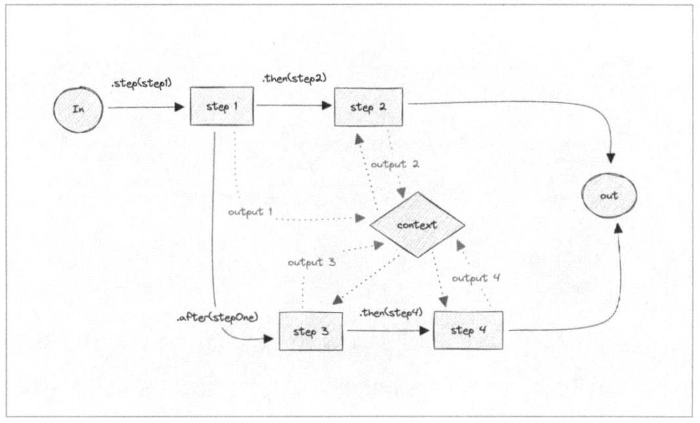

Chaining

This is the simplest operation. Sometimes, you'll want to fetch data from a remote source before you feed it into an LLM, or feed the results of one LLM call into another.

In Mastra, you chain with the `.then()` command. Here's a simple example:

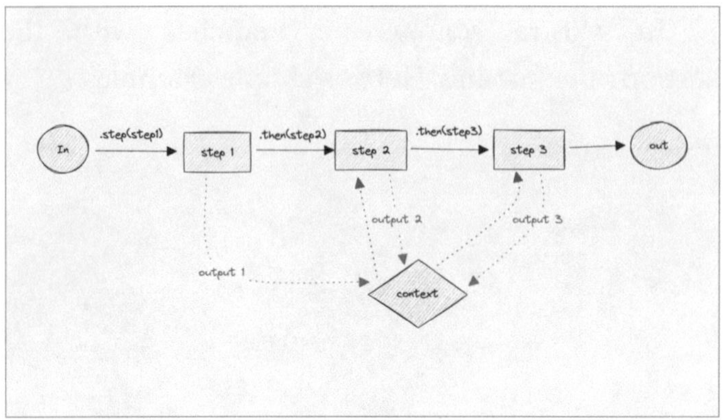

Each step in the chain waits for the previous step to complete, and has access to previous step results via context.

Merging

After branching paths diverge to handle different aspects of a task, they often need to converge again to combine their results:

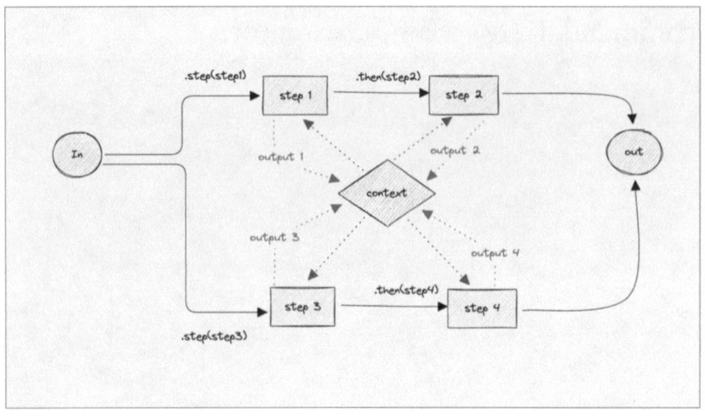

Conditions

Sometimes your workflow needs to make decisions based on intermediate results.

In workflow graphs, because multiple paths can typically execute in parallel, in Mastra we define the conditional path execution on the child step rather than the parent step.

In this example, a `processData` step is executing, conditional on the `fetchData` step succeeding.

```
myWorkflow.step(
  new Step({
    id: "processData",
    execute: async ({ context }) => {
      // Action logic
    },
  }),
  {
    when: {
      "fetchData.status": "success",
    },
  },
);
```

Best Practices and Notes

It's helpful to compose steps in such a way that the input/output at each step is meaningful in some way, since you'll be able to see it in your tracing. (More soon in the *Tracing* section).

Another is to decompose steps in such a way that the LLM only has to do one thing at one time. This usually means no more than one LLM call in any step.

Many different special cases of workflow graphs, like loops, retries, etc can be made by combining these primitives.

14

SUSPEND AND RESUME

Sometimes workflows need to pause execution while waiting for a third-party (like a human-in-the-loop) to provide input.

Because the third party can take arbitrarily long to respond, you don't want to keep a running process.

Instead, you want to persist the state of the workflow, and have some function that you can call to pick up where you left off.

Let's diagram out a simple example with Mastra, which has `.suspend()` and `.resume()` functions:

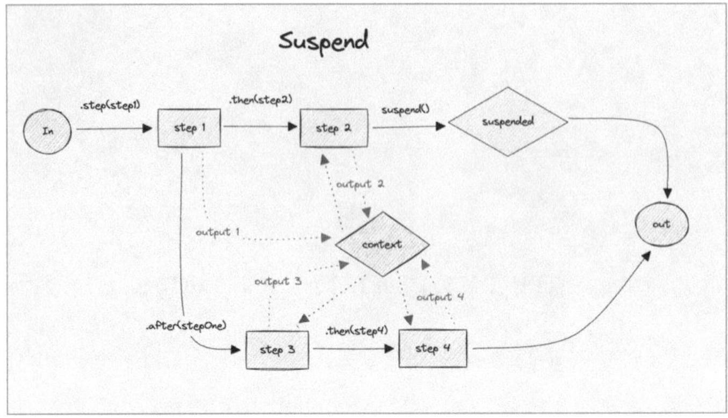

To handle suspended workflows, you can watch for status changes and resume execution when ready:

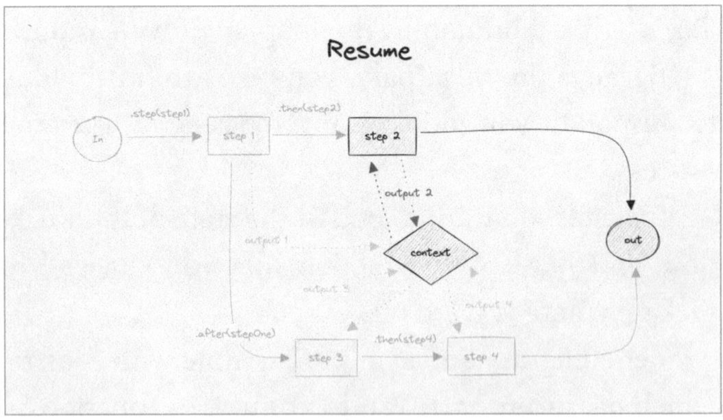

Here's a simple example of creating workflow with `suspend` and `resume` in Mastra.

Steps are the building blocks of workflows. Create a step using `createStep`:

```
// Create a step with defined input/output schemas and execution logic
const inputSchema = z.object({
  inputValue: z.string(),
});

const myStep = createStep({
  id: "my-step",
  description: "Does something useful",
  inputSchema,
  outputSchema: z.object({
    outputValue: z.string(),
  }),
  // Optional: Define the resume schema for step resumption
  resumeSchema: z.object({
    resumeValue: z.string(),
  }),
  // Optional: Define the suspend schema for step suspension
  suspendSchema: z.object({
    suspendValue: z.string(),
  }),
  execute: async ({
    inputData,
    mastra,
    getStepResult,
    getInitData,
    runtimeContext,
  }) => {
    const otherStepOutput = getStepResult(step2);
    const initData = getInitData<typeof inputSchema>(); // typed as the input schema
variable (zod schema)
    return {
      outputValue: `Processed: ${inputData.inputValue}, ${initData.startValue}
(runtimeContextValue: ${runtimeContext.get("runtimeContextValue")})`,
    };
  },
});
```

Then create a workflow using `createWorkflow`:

```
// Create a workflow with defined steps and execution flow
const myWorkflow = createWorkflow({
  id: "my-workflow",
  // Define the expected input structure (should match the first step's inputSchema)
  inputSchema: z.object({
    startValue: z.string(),
  }),
  // Define the expected output structure (should match the last step's outputSchema)
  outputSchema: z.object({
    result: z.string(),
  }),
  steps: [step1, step2, step3], // Declare steps used in this workflow
})
  .then(step1)
  .then(step2)
  .then(step3)
  .commit();

// Register workflow with Mastra instance
const mastra = new Mastra({
  vnext_workflows: {
    myWorkflow,
  },
});

// Create a run instance of the workflow
const run = mastra.vnext_getWorkflow("myWorkflow").createRun();
```

After defining a workflow, run it like so:

```
// Create a run instance
const run = myWorkflow.createRun();

// Start the workflow with input data
const result = await run.start({
  inputData: {
    startValue: "initial data",
  },
});

// Access the results
console.log(result.steps); // All step results
console.log(result.steps["step-id"].output); // Output from a specific step

if (result.status === "success") {
  console.log(result.result); // The final result of the workflow, result of the last
step (or `.map()` output, if used as last step)
} else if (result.status === "suspended") {
  const resumeResult = await run.resume({
    step: result.suspended[0], // there is always at least one step id in the suspended
array, in this case we resume the first suspended execution path
    resumeData: {
      /* user input */
    },
  });
} else if (result.status === "failed") {
  console.error(result.error); // only exists if status is failed, this is an instance of
Error
}
```

15

STREAMING UPDATES

One of the keys to making LLM applications feel fast and responsive is showing users what's happening while the model is working. We've shipped some big improvements here, and our new demo really shows off what modern streaming can do.

Let's revisit my ongoing (and still unsuccessful) quest to plan a Hawaii trip.

Last year, I tried two reasoning models side by side: OpenAI's o1 pro (left tab) and Deep Research (right tab).

The o1 pro just showed a spinning "reasoning" box for three minutes-no feedback, just waiting. Deep Research, on the other hand, immediately asked me for details (number of people, budget, dietary needs), then streamed back updates as it found restaurants and attractions. It felt way snappier and kept me in the loop the whole time.

Left: o1 pro (less good). ***Right:*** *Deep Research (more good)*

The challenge: streaming while functions run

Here's the catch: when you're building LLM agents, you're usually streaming in the middle of a function that expects a certain return type. Sometimes, you have to wait for the whole LLM output before the function can return a result to the user. But what if the function takes ages? This is where things get tricky. Ideally, you want to stream step-by-step progress to the user as soon as you have it, not just dump everything at the end.

A lot of folks are hacking around this. For example, Simon at Assistant UI set up his app to write every token from OpenAI directly to the database as it streamed in, using ElectricSQL to instantly sync those updates to the frontend. This creates a kind of "escape hatch"-even if the function isn't done, the user sees live progress.

Why streaming matters

The most common thing to stream is the LLM's own output (showing tokens as they're generated.) But you can also stream updates from each step in a multi-step workflow or agent pipeline, like when an agent is searching, planning, and summarizing in sequence.

This keeps users engaged and reassured that things are moving along, even if the backend is still crunching.

How to Build This

- **Stream as much as you can:** Whether it's tokens, workflow steps, or custom data, get it to the user ASAP.
- **Use reactive tools:** Libraries like ElectricSQL or frameworks like Turbo Streams make it easier to sync backend updates directly to the UI.
- **Escape hatches:** If your function is stuck waiting, find ways to push partial results or progress updates to the frontend.

Bottom line: Streaming isn't just a nice-to-have-it's critical for good UX in LLM apps. Users want to see progress, not just a blank screen. If you nail this, your agents will feel faster and more reliable, even if the backend is still working hard.

Now, if only streaming could help me actually get to Hawaii...

16

OBSERVABILITY AND TRACING

Because LLMs are non-deterministic, the question isn't *whether* your application will go off the rails.

It's *when* and *how much*.

Teams that have shipped agents into production typically talk about how important it is to look at production data for every step, of every run, of each of their workflows.

Agent frameworks like Mastra that let you write your code as structured workflow graphs will also emit telemetry that enables this.

Observability

Observability is a word that gets a lot of airplay, but since its meaning has been largely diluted and generalized by self-interested vendors let's go to the root.

The initial term was popularized by Honeycomb's Charity Majors in the late 2010s to describe the quality of being able to visualize application traces.

Tracing

To debug a function, it would be *really nice* to be able to see the input and output of every function it called. And the input and output of every function *those* functions called. (And so on, and so on, turtles all the way down.)

This kind of telemetry is called a *trace*, which is made up of a tree of *spans.* (Think about a nested HTML document, or a flame chart.)

The standard format for traces is known as OpenTelemetry, or OTel for short. When monitoring vendors began supporting tracing, each had a different spec — there was no portability. Lightstep's Ben Sigelman helped create the common Otel standard, and larger vendors like Datadog (under duress) began to support Otel.

There's a large number of observability vendors, both older backend and AI-specific ones, but the UI patterns converge:

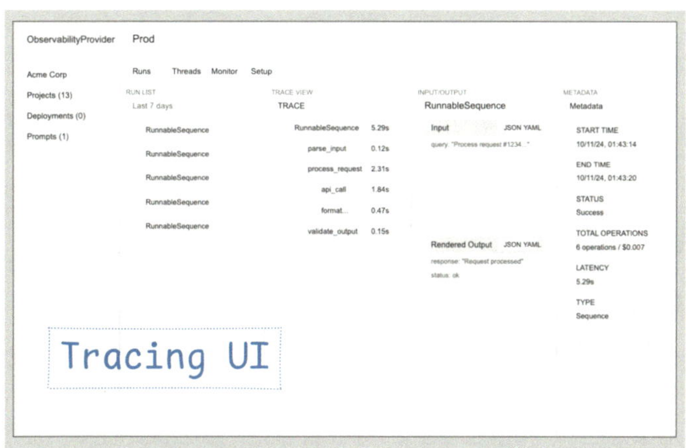

A sample tracing screen

What this sort of UI screen gives you is:

- **A trace view.** This shows how long each step in the pipeline took (e.g., parse_input, process_request, api_call, etc.)
- **Input/output inspection.** Seeing the exact "Input" and "Output" in JSON is helpful for debugging data flowing into and out of Lams
- **Call metadata.** Showing status, start/end times, latency, etc.) provides key context around each run, helping humans scanning for anomalies.

Evals

It's also nice to be able to see your evals (more on evals later) in a cloud environment.

For each of their evals, people want to see a side-by-side comparison of what how the agent responded versus what was expected.

They want to see the overall score on each PR (to ensure there aren't regressions), and the score over time, and to filter by tags, run date, and so on.

Eval UIs tends to look like this:

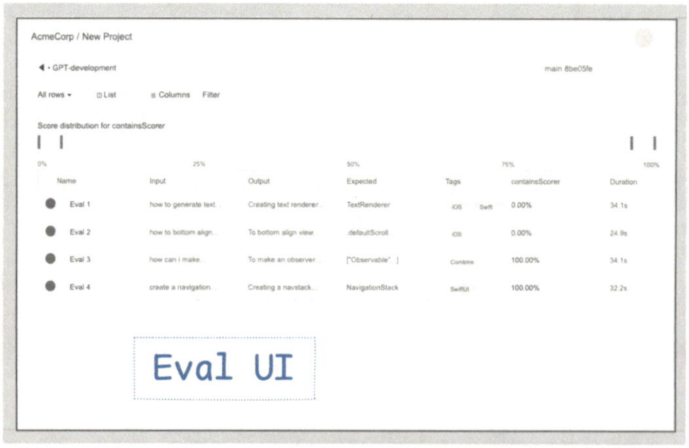

A sample evaluation screen

Final notes on observability and tracing

- You'll need a cloud tool to view this sort of data for your production app.

- It's *also* nice to be able to look at this data locally when you're developing (Mastra does this). More on this in the local development section.
- There is a common standard called OpenTelemetry, or OTel for short, and we strongly recommend emitting in that format.

PART V

RETRIEVAL-AUGMENTED GENERATION (RAG)

17

RAG 101

RAG lets agents ingest user data and synthesize it with their global knowledge base to give users high quality responses.

Here's how it works.

Chunking: You start by taking a document (although we can use other kinds of sources as well) and chunking it. We want to split the document into bite-sized pieces for search.

Embedding: After chunking, you'll want to embed your data – transform it into a vector, or an array of 1536 values between 0 and 1, representing the meaning of the text.

We do this with LLMs, because they make the embeddings much more accurate; OpenAI has an API for this, there are other providers like Voyage or Cohere.

You need to use a vector DB which can store

these vectors and do the math to search on them. You can use pgvector, which comes out of the box with Postgres.

Indexing: Once you pick a vector DB, you need to set up an index to store your document chunks, represented as vector embeddings.

Querying: Okay, after that setup, you can now query the database!

Under the hood, you'll be running an algorithm that compares your query string to all the chunks in the database and returning the most similar ones. The most popular algorithm is called "cosine similarity".

The implementation is similar to a geospatial query searching latitude/longitude, except the search goes over 1536 dimensions instead of two.

You can use other algorithms as well.

Reranking: Optionally, after querying, you can use a reranker. Reranking is a more computationally expensive way of searching the dataset. You can run it over your results to improve the ordering (but it would take too long to run it over the entire database).

Synthesis: finally, you pass your results as context into an LLM, along with any other context you way, and it can synthesize an answer to the user.

18

CHOOSING A VECTOR DATABASE

One of the biggest questions people having around RAG is how they should think of a vector DB.

There are multiple form factors of vector databases:

1. A feature on top of open-source databases (**pgvector** on top of Postgres, the **libsql vector store**)
2. Standalone open-source (**Chroma**)
3. Standalone hosted cloud service (**Pinecone**).
4. Hosted by an existing cloud provider (**Cloudflare Vectorize, DataStax Astra**).

Our take is that unless your use-case is exceptionally specialized, the vector DB feature set is mostly commoditized.

Back in 2023, VC funding drove a huge explosion in vector DB companies, which while exciting for the space as a whole, created a whole set of competing solutions with little differentiation.

Today, in practice teams report that the most important thing is to prevent infra sprawl (yet *another* service to maintain). Our recommendation:

- If you're already using Postgres for your app backend, pgvector is a great choice.
- If you're spinning up a new project, Pinecone is a default choice with a nice UI.
- If your cloud provider has a managed vector DB service, use that.

19

SETTING UP YOUR RAG PIPELINE

Chunking

Chunking is the process of breaking down large documents into smaller, manageable pieces for processing.

The key thing you'll need to choose here is a **strategy** and an **overlap window.** Good chunking balances context preservation with retrieval granularity.

Chunking strategies including recursive, character-based, token-aware, and format-specific (Markdown, HTML, JSON, LaTeX) splitting. Mastra supports all of them.

Embedding

Embeddings are numerical representations of text that capture semantic meaning. These vectors allow us to perform similarity searches. Mastra supports multiple embedding providers like OpenAI and Cohere, with the ability to generate embeddings for both individual chunks and arrays of text.

Upsert

Upsert operations allow you to insert or update vectors and their associated metadata in your vector store. This operation is essential for maintaining your knowledge base, combining both the embedding vectors and any additional metadata that might be useful for retrieval.

Indexing

An index is a data structure that optimizes vector similarity search. When creating an index, you specify parameters like dimension size (matching your embedding model) and similarity metric (cosine, euclidean, dot product). This is a one-time setup step for each collection of vectors.

Querying

Querying involves converting user input into an embedding and finding similar vectors in your vector store. The basic query returns the most semantically similar chunks to your input, typically with a similarity score. Under the hood, this is a bunch of matrix multiplication to find the closest point in *n-*dimensional space (think about a geo search with lat/lng, except in 1536 dimensions instead).

The most common algorithm that does this is called *cosine similarity* (although you can use others instead).

> **Hybrid Queries with Metadata.** Hybrid queries combine vector similarity search with traditional metadata filtering. This allows you to narrow down results based on both semantic similarity and structured metadata fields like dates, categories, or custom attributes.

Reranking

Reranking is a post-processing step that improves result relevance by applying more sophisticated scoring methods. It considers factors like semantic relevance, vector similarity, and position bias to reorder results for better accuracy.

It's a more computationally intense process, so you typically don't want to run it over your entire corpus for latency reasons — you'll typically just run it on a code example.

Code Example

Here's some code using Mastra to set up a RAG pipeline. Mastra includes a consistent interface for creating indexes, upserting embeddings, and querying, while offering their own unique features and optimizations, so while this example uses Pinecone, you could easily use another DB instead.

```
import { Mastra } from "@mastra/core";
import { MDocument, PgVector } from "@mastra/rag";
import { embedMany, embed } from "ai";
import { openai } from "@ai-sdk/openai";

// Initialize document and create chunks
const doc = MDocument.fromText(`Your text content here...`);
const chunks = await doc.chunk({
  strategy: "recursive",
  size: 512,
  overlap: 50,
});

// Generate embeddings
const { embeddings } = await embedMany({
  values: chunks.map(chunk => chunk.text),
  model: openai.embedding("text-embedding-3-small"),
});

// Initialize vector store and Mastra
const pgVector = new PgVector(process.env.POSTGRES_CONNECTION_STRING!);
const mastra = new Mastra({ vectors: { pgVector } });

// Store embeddings
await pgVector.createIndex("embeddings", 1536);
await pgVector.upsert(
  "embeddings",
  embeddings,
  chunks?.map(chunk => ({ text: chunk.text }))
);

// Query example
const query = "insert query here";
const { embedding } = await embed({
  value: query,
  model: openai.embedding("text-embedding-3-small"),
});

// Retrieve similar chunks
const results = await pgVector.query("embeddings", embedding);
const relevantContext = results
  .map(result => result?.metadata?.text)
  .join("\n\n");

// Generate response
const completion = await openai("gpt-4o-mini").generate(`
  Please answer the following question:
  ${query}

  Based on this context: ${relevantContext}
  If the context lacks sufficient information, please state that
explicitly.

console.log(completion.text);
```

Note: There are advanced ways of doing RAG: using LLMs to generate metadata, using LLMs to refine search queries; using graph databases to model complex relationships. These may be useful for you, but start by setting up a working pipeline and tweaking the normal parameters — embedding models, rerankers, chunking algorithms — first.

20

ALTERNATIVES TO RAG

Great, know you know how RAG works. But does it matter? Or, put like a Twitter edgelord, is RAG dead?

Not yet, we think. But there are some simpler approaches you should probably reach for first before setting up a RAG pipeline.

Agentic RAG

Instead of searching through documents, you can give your agent a set of tools to help it reason about a domain. For example, a financial advisor agent might have access to market data APIs, calculators, and portfolio analysis tools. The agent can then use these tools to generate more accurate and grounded responses.

The advantage of agentic RAG is that it can be

more precise than RAG - rather than searching for relevant text, the agent can compute exact answers. The downside is that you need to build and maintain the tools, and the agent needs to know how to use them effectively.

One of our investors built a variety of tools to query her website in various ways, and then bundled them into a MCP server she could give to the Windsurf agent.

She then recorded a demo where she asked the agent about her favorite restaurants (it recommended Flour + Water in San Francisco) and her favorite portfolio companies (it demurred, saying she likes all of her companies equally). *

Reasoning-Augmented Generation (ReAG)

ReAG is a loose grouping of thought that focuses on improving using models to enrich text chunks.

ReAG advocates say you should think about what you would do with 10x your LLM budget to improve your RAG pipeline quality — then go do it. They point out that pre-processing is asynchronous, so it doesn't need to be fast.

Some thought experiments to consider if you're thinking about ReAG:

* Code available at https://github.com/alanagoyal/mcp-server

- when you're annotating, send a request to a model 10x at high temperature to see if the responses have consensus.
- send the input through an LLM before retrieving data
- extract rich semantic information, including references to other sections, entity names, and any structured relationships

Full Context Loading

With newer models supporting larger context windows (Gemini has 2m tokens), sometimes the simplest approach is to just load all the relevant content directly into the context. This works particularly well with models optimized for reasoning over long contexts, like Claude or GPT-4.

The advantages are simplicity and reliability - no need to worry about chunking or retrieval, and the model can see all the context at once. The main limitations are:

- Cost (you pay for the full context window)
- Size constraints (even large windows have limits)
- Potential for distraction (the model might focus on irrelevant parts)

Conclusion

We're engineers. And engineers can over-engineer things.

With RAG, you should fight that tendency. Start simple, check quality, get complex.

Step one, you should be throwing your entire corpus into Gemini's context window. Step two, write a bunch of functions to access your dataset, bundle them in an MCP server, and give them to the Cursor or Windsurf agent.

If neither step one or step two give you good enough quality, *then* consider building a RAG pipeline.

PART VI

MULTI-AGENT SYSTEMS

21

MULTI-AGENT 101

Think about a multi-agent systems like a specialized team, like marketing or engineering, at a company. Different AI agents work together, each with their own specialized role, to ultimately accomplish more complex tasks.

Interestingly, if you've used a code-generation tool like Replit agent that's deployed in production, you've actually already been using a multi-agent system.

One agent works with you to plan / architect your code. After you've worked with the agent to plan it out, you work with a "code manager" agent that passes instructions to a code writer, then executes the resulting code in a sandbox and passes any errors back to the code writer.

Each of these agents has different memories,

different system prompts, and access to different tools.

We often joke that designing a multi-agent system involves a lot of skills used in organizational design. You try to group related tasks into a job description where you could plausibly recruit someone. You might give creative or generative tasks to one person and review or analytical tasks to another.

You want to think about network dynamics. Is it better for three specialized agents to gossip among themselves until consensus is reached? Or feed their output back to a manager agent who can make a decision?

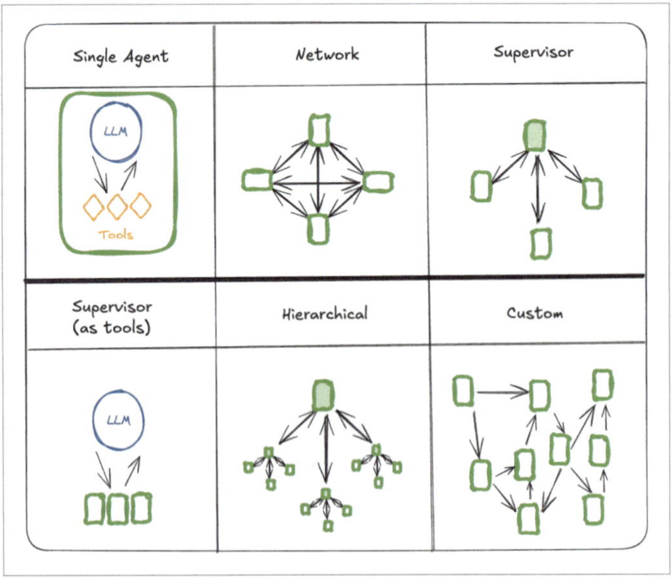

One advantage of multi-agent systems is

breaking down complex tasks into manageable pieces. And of course, designs are fractal. A hierarchy is just a supervisor of supervisors. But start with the simplest version first.

Let's break down some of the patterns.

22

AGENT SUPERVISOR

Agent supervisors are specialized agents that coordinate and manage other agents. The most straightforward way to do this is to pass in the other agents wrapped as tools.

For example, in a content creation system, a publisher agent might supervise both a copywriter and an editor:

```
const publisherAgent = new Agent({
  name: "publisherAgent",
  instructions: "You are a publisher agent that coordinates content creation. First call the copywriter for initial content, then the editor for refinement.",
  model: {
    provider: "ANTHROPIC",
    name: "claude-3-5-sonnet-20241022",
  },
  tools: { copywriterTool, editorTool },
});
```

23

CONTROL FLOW

When building complex AI applications, you need a structured way to manage how agents think and work through tasks. Just as a project manager wouldn't start coding without a plan, agents should establish an approach before diving into execution.

Just like how it's common practice for PMs to spec out features, get stakeholder approval, and only then commission engineering work, you shouldn't expect to work with agents without first aligning on what the desired work is.

We recommend engaging with your agents on architectural details first — and perhaps adding a few checkpoints for human feedback in their workflows.

24

WORKFLOWS AS TOOLS

Hopefully, by now, you're starting to see that all multi-agent architecture comes down to which primitive you're using and how you're arranging them.

It's particularly important to remember this framing when trying to build more complex tasks into agents.

Let's say you want your agent(s) to accomplish 3 separate tasks. You can't do this easily in a single LLM call. But you can turn each of those tasks into individual workflows. There's more certainty in doing it this way because you can stipulate a workflow's order of steps and provide more structure.

Each of these workflows can then be passed along as *tools* to the agent(s).

25

COMBINING THE PATTERNS

If you've played around with code writing tools like Repl.it and Lovable.dev, you'll notice that they have planning agents and a code writing agent. (And in fact the code writing agent is two different agents, a reviewer and writer that work together.)

It's critical for these tools to have planning agents if they're to create any good deliverables for you at all.

The planning agent proposes an architecture for the app you desire. It asks you, "how does that sound?"

You get to give it feedback until you and the agent are aligned enough on the plan such that it can pass it along to the code writing agents.

In this example, *agents embody different steps in a*

workflow. They are responsible either for planning, coding, or review and each work in a specific order.

In the previous example, you'll notice that workflows are steps (tools) for agents. These are inverse examples to one another, which brings us, again, to an important takeaway.

All the primitives can be rearranged in the way you want, custom to the control flow you want.

26

MULTI-AGENT STANDARDS

While it hasn't enjoyed quite the rapid liftoff of Anthropic's MCP, the other protocol that's gained speed in spring 2025 is Google's A2A.

While all the multi-agent material we've covered so far relates to how you'd orchestrate multiple agents assuming you controlled all of them, A2A is a protocol for communicating with "untrusted" agents.

Like MCP, A2A solves an *n x n* problem. If there are *n* different agents, each of which uses a different framework, you would have to write *n x m* different integrations to make them work together.

How A2A works

A2A relies on a JSON metadata file hosted at `/.well-known/agent.json` that describes what the agent can do, its endpoint URL, and authentication requirements.

Once authorization happens, and assuming the agents have implemented the A2A client and server protocols, they can send tasks to each other with a queueing system.

Tasks have unique IDs and progress through states like submitted, working, input-required, completed, failed, or canceled. A2A supports both synchronous request-response patterns and streaming for longer-running tasks using Server-Sent Events.

Communication happens over HTTP and JSON-RPC 2.0, with messages containing parts (text, files, or structured data). Agents can generate artifacts as outputs and send real-time updates via server-side events. Communication uses standard web auth — OAuth, API keys, HTTP codes, and so on.

A2A vs. MCP

A2A is younger than MCP, and while Microsoft supports A2A, neither OpenAI nor Anthropic has jumped on board. It's possible they view MCP as competitive to A2A. Time will tell.

Either way, expect one or multiple agent interoperability protocol from the big players to emerge as the default standard.

PART VII

EVALS

27

EVALS 101

While traditional software tests have clear pass/fail conditions, AI outputs are non-deterministic — they can vary with the same input. Evals help bridge this gap by providing quantifiable metrics for measuring agent quality.

Instead of binary pass/fail results, evals return scores between 0 and 1.

Think about evals sort of like including, say, performance testing in your CI pipeline. There's going to be some randomness in each result, but on the whole and over time there should be a correlation between application performance and test results.

When writing evals, it's important to think about what *exactly* you want to test.

There are different kinds of evals just like there are different kinds of tests.

Unit tests are easy to write and run but might not capture the behavior that matters; end-to-end tests might capture the right behavior but they might be more flaky.

Similarly, if you're building a RAG pipeline, or a structured workflow, you may want to test each step along the way, and then after that test the behavior of the system as a whole.

28

TEXTUAL EVALS

Textual evals can feel a bit like a grad student TA grading your homework with a rubric. They are going to be a bit pedantic, but they usually have a point.

Accuracy and reliability

You can evaluate how correct, truthful, and complete your agent's answers are. For example:

- **Hallucination.** Do responses contain facts or claims not present in the provided context? This is especially important for RAG applications.
- **Faithfulness.** Do responses accurately represent provided context?

- **Content similarity.** Do responses maintain consistent information across different phrasings?
- **Completeness.** Do response includes all necessary information from the input or context?
- **Answer relevancy.** How well do responses address the original query?

Understanding context

You can evaluate how well your agent is using provided context, eg retrieved excerpts from sources, facts and statistics, and user details added to context. For example:

- **Context position.** Where does context appears in responses? (Usually the correct position for context is at the top.)
- **Context precision.** Are context chunks grouped logically? Does the response maintains the original meaning?
- **Context relevancy.** Does the response uses the most appropriate pieces of context?
- **Contextual recall.** Does the response completely "recall" context provided?

Output

You can evaluate **how well the model delivers** its final answer in line with requirements around format, style, clarity, and alignment.

- **Tone consistency**. Do responses maintain the correct level of formality, technical complexity, emotional tone, and style?
- **Prompt Alignment.** Do responses follow explicit instructions like length restrictions, required elements, and specific formatting requirements?
- **Summarization Quality.** Do responses condense information accurately? Consider eg information retention, factual accuracy, and conciseness?
- **Keyword Coverage.** Does a response include technical terms and terminology use?

Other output eval metrics like toxicity & bias detection are important but largely baked into leading models.

Code Example

Here's an example with three different evaluation metrics that automatically check a content writing agent's output for accuracy, faithfulness to source material, and potential hallucinations:

```
import { Agent } from "@mastra/core/agent";
import { openai } from "@ai-sdk/openai";
import {
  FaithfulnessMetric,
  ContentSimilarityMetric,
  HallucinationMetric
} from "@mastra/evals/nlp";

// Configure the agent with the evals array
export const myAgent = new Agent({
  name: "ContentWriter",
  instructions: "You are a content writer that creates accurate
summdelesopenai("gpt-4o"),
  evals: [
      new FaithfulnessMetric(), // Checks if output matches source material
      new ContentSimilarityMetric({
        threshold: 0.8 // Require 80% similarity with expected output
      }),
      new HallucinationMetric()
    ];
});
```

29

OTHER EVALS

There are a few other types of evals as well.

Classification or Labeling Evals

Classification or labeling evals help determine how accurately a model tags or categorizes data based on predefined categories (e.g., sentiment, topics, spam vs. not spam).

This can include broad labeling tasks (like recognizing document intent) or fine-grained tasks (like identifying specific entities aka entity extraction).

Agent Tool Usage Evals

Tool usage or agent evals measure how effectively a model or agent calls external tools or APIs to solve problems.

For example, like you would write `expect(Fn).toBeCalled` in the JavaScript testing framework Jest, you would want similar functions for agent tool use.

Prompt Engineering Evals

Prompt engineering evals explore how different instructions, formats, or phrasings of user queries impact an agent's performance.

They look at both the **sensitivity** of the agent to prompt variations (whether small changes produce large differences in results) and the **robustness** to adversarial or ambiguous inputs.

All things "prompt injection" fall in this category.

A/B testing

After you launch, depending on your traffic, it's quite plausible to run **live experiments** with real users to compare two versions of your system.

In fact, leaders of larger consumer and developer tools AI companies, like Perplexity and Replit, joke that they rely more on A/B testing of user metrics than evals per se. They have enough traffic that degradation in agent quality will be quickly visible.

Human data review

In addition to automated tests, high-performing AI teams regularly review production data. Typically, the easiest way to do this is to view traces which capture the input and output of each step in the pipeline. We discussed this earlier in the *workflows* and *deployment* section.

Many correctness aspects (e.g., subtle domain knowledge, or an unusual user request) can't be fully captured by rigid assertions, but human eyes catch these nuances.

PART VIII

DEVELOPMENT & DEPLOYMENT

30

LOCAL DEVELOPMENT

gent development typically falls into two different categories: building the frontend and the backend.

Building an agentic web frontend

Web-based agent frontends tend to share a few characteristics: they're built around a chat interface, stream to a backend, autoscroll, display tool calls.

We discussed the importance of streaming in an earlier chapter. Agentic interfaces tend using a variety of different transport options like request/response, server-sent events, webhooks and web sockets, all to feed the sense of real-time interactivity.

There are a few frameworks we see speeding up development here, especially during the prototype phase: Assistant UI, Copilot Kit, and Vercel's AI SDK UI.

(And many agents are based on other platforms like WhatsApp, Slack, or email and don't have a web frontend!)

It's important to note that while agentic frontends can be powerful, the full agent logic generally can't live client-side in the browser for security reasons — it would leak your API keys to LLM providers.

Building an agent backend

So it's the backend where we typically see most of the complexity.

When developing AI applications, it's important to see what your agents are doing, make sure your tools work, and be able to quickly iterate on your prompts.

Some things that we've seen be helpful for a local agent development:

- **Agent Chat Interface:** Test conversations with your agents in the browser, seeing how they respond to different inputs and use their configured tools.
- **Workflow Visualizer:** Seeing step-by-step workflow execution and being able to suspend/resume/replay

- **Agent/workflow endpoints:** Being able to curl agents and workflows on localhost (this also enables using eg Postman)
- **Tool Playground:** Testing any tools and being able to verify inputs / outputs without needing to invoke them through an agent.
- **Tracing & Evals:** See inputs and outputs of each step of agent and workflow execution, as well as eval metrics as you iterate on code.

Here's a screenshot from Mastra's local dev environment:

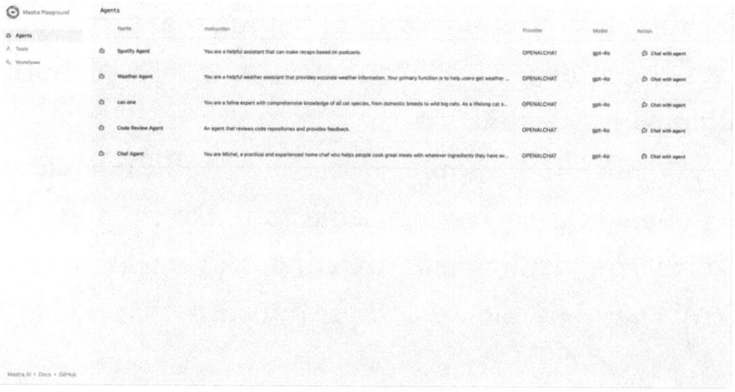

31

DEPLOYMENT

In May 2025, we're still generally in the Heroku era of agent deployment.

Most teams are putting their agents into some sort of web server, then putting that server into a Docker image and deploying it onto a platform that will scale that.

While web applications are well-understood enough that we've been able to make progress on serverless deployment paradigms (Vercel, Render, AWS Lambda, etc), agents are not yet at that point.

Deployment challenges

Relative to typical web request/response cycles, agent workloads are somewhat more complicated.

They are often long-running, similar to the workloads on durable execution engines like

Temporal and Inngest. But they are still tied to a specific user request.

Run on serverless platforms, the long-running processes can cause function timeouts. In addition, bundle sizes can be too large, and some serverless hosts don't support the full Node.js runtime.

Using a managed platform

The agent teams sleeping the soundest at night are the ones we see who figure out how to run their agents using auto-scaling managed services.

Serverless providers (generally) aren't there yet — long-running processes can cause function timeouts, and bundle sizes are a problem.

Teams using container services like AWS EC2, Digital Ocean, or equivalent seem to be all right as long as they have a B2B use case that won't have sudden usage spikes.

(And of course, at Mastra, we have a beta cloud service with autoscaling)

PART IX

EVERYTHING ELSE

32

MULTIMODAL

One way to think about multimodality (images, video, voice) in AI is to map their dates of origin on various platforms.

Consider the Internet: it supported text from its origin in the 1970s, but images and video weren't supported until the web browser (1992), and voice not until 1995.

Voice and video didn't become popular until YouTube (2002) and Skype (2003), with greater bandwidth and connection speeds.

Or think about social networks: all the early ones, like MySpace (2002), Facebook (2004), and Twitter (2008), were primarily text-based.

Image-based social media didn't become popular until Instagram (2010) and Snapchat (2013), and video-based social media until TikTok (2017).

In AI, then, it's little wonder that multi-modal use-cases are a bit younger and less mature. Like on earlier platforms, they're trickier to get right, and more computationally complex.

Image Generation

March 2025 brought the invention of Ghibli-core — think soft colors, dreamy backgrounds, and those iconic wide-eyed characters.

People had been playing with Midjourney, Stable Diffusion, and others for a while. But March was a step forward in consumer-grade image-generation, with to transpose photos into specific styles.

People uploaded selfies or old photos, added a prompt, and instantly got back an anime version that looked straight out of "Spirited Away."

The Mastra cofounders (Shane, Abhi and Sam) at a basketball game

This wasn't just a niche thing; the Ghibli trend took over social feeds everywhere. The official (Trump) White House account joined the fray by (controversially) tweeted out a Ghibli-fied picture of a detained immigrant.

More broadly, the "Ghibli" moment showed vitality for the digital art use case — image gen for what was something between a storyboard, a character sketch, and environment concepts.

Use Cases

In terms of people using image gen for products, there are a few use-cases.

In marketing and e-commerce, product mockups

on varied backgrounds and rapid ad creative generation without photoshoots and in various form factors. "Try-on" image models allow people to swap out the human model but keep the featured clothing item.

The third use-case for image gen has been in video game and film production. Image gen has allowed for asset prototyping, including portraits, textures, props, as well as scene layout planning via rough "sketch to render" flows.

Put in web development terms, this gives the fidelity of a full design with the effort/skill of a wireframe.

Last, there are more NSFW use-cases. These don't tend to be venture-fundable, but at least according to the Silicon Valley gossip mills, quite a few of the more risqué use-cases print money — if you can find a payment processor that will take your business.

Voice

The key modalities in voice are speech-to-text (STT), text-to-speech (TTS), and speech-to-speech, also known as realtime voice.

What *users want* in an agent voice product is something that can understand their tone, and respond immediately.

In order to do that, you could train a model that

specifically takes voice tokens as input, and responds with voice tokens as output. That's known as "real-time voice", but it's proved challenging.

For one thing, it's difficult to train such models; the information density of audio is only 1/1000 of text, so these models take significantly more input data to train and cost more to serve.

Second, these models still struggle with turn-taking, known in the industry as "voice activity detection". When talking, humans interrupt each other constantly using both visual and emotional cues.

But voice models don't have these cues, and have to deal with both computational and network latency. When they interrupt too early, they cut people off; when they interrupt too late, they sound robotic.

While these products make great demos, there are not too many companies using realtime voice in production.

What they use instead is speech-to-text (STT) and text-to-speech (TTS) pipeline. They use one model to translate input voice to text, another model to generate response text, and then translate the response text into an audio response.

Here's an example of listening; you could follow this up with `agent.speak()` to reply.

```
import { Agent } from "@mastra/core/agent";
import { OpenAIVoice } from "@mastra/voice-openai";

const agent = new Agent({
  name: 'Agent',
  instructions: `You are a helpful assistant with
voice capabilities.`,
  model: openai('gpt-4o'),
  voice: new OpenAIVoice();
});

const audioStream =
fs.createReadStream('/path/to.mp3')

const text = await agent.listen(audioStream)

// Hey! How are ya!
```

Video

AI video generation products, while exciting, have not yet crossed from machine learning into AI engineering.

Consumer models have not yet had their Studio Ghibli moment where they can accurately represent characters in input and replay them in alternate settings.

As a result, products tend require a lot of specialized knowledge to build, and consume GPU cycles on runtime generating avatars from user input that can then be replayed in new settings and scenarios.

33

CODE GENERATION

With the takeoff of companies like bolt.new and Lovable, as well as coding agent releases in the span of a week from OpenAI, Microsoft, and Google, have come a surge of people interested in building their own coding agents.

Giving your agent code generation tools unlocks powerful workflows, but also comes with important safety and quality considerations.

So, consider the following:

- **Feedback Loops:** Agents can write code, run it, and analyze the results. For example, if the code throws an error, the agent can read the error message and try again—enabling iterative improvement.

- **Sandboxing:** Always run generated code in a sandboxed environment. This prevents the agent from accidentally (or maliciously) running dangerous commands on your machine (like `rm -rf /`).
- **Code Analysis:** You can give agents access to linters, static type checkers, and other analysis tools. This provides ground truth feedback and helps agents write higher-quality code.

If you're building a code agent, you should take a deep look at the tools and platforms that specialize specifically in this use case.

34

WHAT'S NEXT

The agent space is moving incredibly quickly.

We don't have a crystal ball, but from our vantage point as a prominent agent framework, here's what we see:

- **Reasoning models will continue to get better.** Agents like Windsurf and Cursor can plug in Claude 3.7, o4-mini-high, and Claude 4, and improve performance significantly. But what do agents *built* for reasoning models look like? We're not sure.
- **We'll make progress on agent learning.** Agents emit traces, but right now the feedback loop to improve their

performance runs through their human programmers. Different teams are working on different approaches to agent learning (eg supervised fine-tuning as a service). But it's still unclear what the right approach is.

- **Synthetic evals.** Right now, writing evals is an intense, human driven process. Some products are synthetically generating evals from tracing data, with human approval, for specialized use cases. We expect that to expand over the next few months.
- **Security will become more important.** As I'm writing these words, I'm reading about a vulnerability in the official Github MCP server that will leak private repos, API credentials, and so on.. The number of deployed agents will probably 10x or 100x over the next few months, and we'll see more incidents like these.
- **The eternal September of AI will continue.** Every month brings new developers who haven't learned how to write good prompts or what a vector database is. Meanwhile, the rapid pace of model updates means even established teams are constantly adapting their

implementations. In a field where the ground shift constantly, we're all perpetual beginners. To build something enduring, you have to stay humble.

Made in the USA
Columbia, SC
10 June 2025